The VICTORIOUS WIDOW
STORIES OF LOSS, OVERCOMING AND RESILIENCE

PRESENTED BY:
EVELYN DONELSON

KP
KILGORE PUBLISHING

FLINT MICHIGAN

The Victorious Widow: Stories of Loss, Overcoming and Resilience

Copyright © 2021 by Kilgore Publishing

All rights are reserved. Except as permitted under the U.S. Copyright Act of 1976, no part of the publication may be reproduced, distributed, or transmitted in any form or by any means, or stored in a database or retrieval system without the prior written permission of the publisher.

This book is available in volume for qualifying organizations. Please contact the visionary to inquire evelutionconsulting@ail.com.

For more information about this book, or speaking engagements please email evelutionconsulting@ail.com.

Flint Michigan

Since 2015

ISBN : 978-1-7364325-3-2

For Worldwide Distribution Printed in the U.S.

Contents

Dedication 4

Foreword 5

Preface 6

Introduction 7

Chapter 1 Traumas Birthed My Triumphs 10

Chapter 2 Beautifully Broken 18

Chapter 3 Covid Didn't Break Me 26

Chapter 4 My Wonderful Life 35

Chapter 5 Life Without Him 45

Chapter 6 Catapulted Into Widowhood 53

Chapter 7 Pain To Purpose 61

Chapter 8 The Loss After The Loss 69

Outro Victorious Widow 77

Author Bios 80

Dedication

We would like to dedicate this book to all the women who have gone through, is going through or will go through the healing process after the loss of their spouse. This journey will not be easy but know that you are VICTORIOUS!

Foreword

I learned there are "Five Stages of Grief," which are: denial, anger, bargaining, depression and then acceptance. I watched Evelyn go through not just losing one husband but two. Yes, she is a two-time widow. I admire her strength. I would often ask her, "How do you get through losing someone that was so close to you?" She would say, "By the grace of God. If I didn't have Him by my side, I don't know where I would be." Evelyn has a natural talent for inspiring others to dig deep within themselves to discover their purpose. I believe that is why it was so important for her to connect with other women who were going through the same struggle. Although they had shared losing a husband, each of their journeys were different, but with a common goal- to heal. As you read this book you will find stories that will touch you and deepen your empathy for others.

With Love,

Lisa LaRue

Preface

All of the stories written in this book are true and come from a very delicate place in our hearts. The events touched upon were predominant over our lives until we decided to write and take back the power and become victorious! Our hope is that each person that picks up this book is looking for a way to victory after a loss. We, The Victorious Widows, wanted to share our trials of grief and overcoming so that others can find peace through their storms.

Introduction

The shoulders I stand on TODAY are those of the widows from who I've drawn my strength over the last two years. The tears, anxiety, and pressure we endured through this journey are an understatement. Where we are today is the epitome of victory. Each author in this book brings a unique event of evolution and their very own adventures into being a Victorious Widow. I didn't think I would have ever written about my two losses, hoping to put that hurt behind me. But here I am, and I brought a few victorious widows with me.

We sometimes fail to realize that there is a purpose to our pain, that what we go through will eventually help someone else. This book is about helping women move forward after loss, sharing our stories to uplift and encourage. Someone will read these stories and be inspired to tell their own. Someone will read these stories and overcome the battle of feeling like they've lost everything. You're not alone!

I am very proud to see that I've ignited the writers in these women who have lost, grieved, and overcame the most challenging season in their lives. You will follow their journey of resilience as you read their chapters. As you unfold each page, you will discover that a part of your lives in the seams of the words. You will be pulled into the magnitude of winning! I am a Victorious Widow, they are Victorious Widows, and you are VICTORIOUS!

The
VICTORIOUS WIDOW

CHAPTER

Traumas Birthed My Triumphs

LaTasha McCollum-Hicks

MY UNEXPECTED TRAUMA

After 12 years of marriage, I would never think that this sudden and unexpected situation could happen to me. I never thought I would lose my spouse, best friend, confidant, partner in crime, prayer partner, leaning post, and shoulder to cry on. I never thought he would go so soon due to sudden heart failure. This is why it is so important to cherish every moment with your loved ones because you never know when it will be the last time you will ever see them. I never knew that this could happen to me. He was so noble and overprotective of me. He would not allow me to pick up one bag and carry it into the house.

The worse day of my life all started on March 16, 2020. After hearing the doctor say, *"we have a pulse,"* but then minutes later, hearing the doctor says, *"he's being transferred to another hospital,"* this is when my faith diminished. When the doctor said those words to me, my head dropped, and the tears came rolling down like rivers of water. At that time, I began to cry out to God, pleading and begging him to save him. I was still crying and trying to stay calm while being transported to the second hospital. I couldn't do anything at the time except calm myself down to sing and pray with him. If it had not been for a few church members from that area in Tennessee who came up to both hospitals, I don't know how I would have made it emotionally. As I was transported to the second hospital with ER, the driver, and the crew, I found myself still trying to stay calm. It was another night of my husband fighting for his life, breathing every breath, yet little by little, his breath was leaving. After praying with him, singing to him, still speaking to him, hours later, it was the news my in-laws and I did not want to hear. Everyone accepted the news except me when the chaplain came in and we were notified he was dead. At the time, I was in denial, telling the doctor he was not dead. I told the doctor they all needed to do all they could to revive him. Afterward, I just broke down, weeping, gasping for air, yet still in disbelief.

All of this occurred a week before COVID-19 hit the US in full force. With the comfort and consolation from nearby members of my church, I begin to feel somewhat better. However, I was still facing disbelief and complete brokenness. What was supposed to be a joyous event turned out to be the worst time in my life. I reflect back to even before we left. I kept saying, *"Babe, I'm not feeling this trip. Can you check with them to see if it's still on?"* He responded, *"I think it's still on or they would have told me something different."* This was right after a tumultuous storm and tornado had swept through the state of Tennessee. My heart was troubled, my mind was not at ease, and my spirit encountered bad vibes about the trip to Nashville. My mind, spirit, and heart were not at ease even when we got to the airport. While my mind was telling me that he was feeling alright, my spirit was telling me something was beginning to trouble him. Sometimes God gives you signs that a loved one is soon to transition out of this world. You can clearly see the signs but then not really see and notice that they are indications that the Lord is showing you beforehand. As I look back close to a year before my husband's passing, I could see what was about to unfold right before my eyes without knowing it would be him leaving me. Within a year I had a dream that one of my father's brothers was having heart problems while on the floor, fighting for his life. I was trying to wake up my uncle in the dream (he was deceased years before my husband passed). I woke up shaking, crying outloud, *"Jesus."* After comparing the dream to reality, I realized what was a dream was actually reality in the same way I witnessed my husband's tragedy. This was indeed a revelation from God, and I had no idea it was going to take place a year later. When there is a sense of closeness, closer intimacy, more spending time with each other and forsaking all others, taking so many things in stride, and the two taking a more divine relationship with the Lord, this is when strange things begin to occur.

MY UNEXPECTED TRIUMPH:

After suffering from heavy stages of grief from March 2020 to June 2020, there was a supernatural occurrence I began to experience from God. I went from emotional pain to praise in my sleep and my dreams. I transitioned from emotional and mental struggles to unconditional strength from God. He carried me through even in times I almost lost my mind. I never knew the level of stability God gave me, along with the prayers of many others from family, friends, and church members. Yes, there were times where I wanted to leave this world, the challenges of life, and just say to the Lord, *"Lord, take me."* My heart felt like there was a complete hole in it. Like it was completely shattered, and the only one that could mend it back together again was the Lord. However, after having many encounters with the Lord, he began to let me know my time was not over yet. My purpose had to be fulfilled and my winning season had to come to fruition. I still didn't want to accept that the Lord let me live and my spouse die. There were times where I did not question God but would question my late husband and ask him, *"Why did you leave me?"* and *"What did I do?"* Not only did he show me through dreams, but he stated to me some of the reasons why. On one occasion, he simply responded to me *"Greater."* On another occasion, he said he wanted me to move on and push forward. He often said, *"Tasha, stop all of that crying."* Not accepting his responses, I felt emotionally overwhelmed and cried with a spirit of heaviness.

July 2020, my life was spiritually transitioned from unexpected trauma to unexpected triumph. My healing process took place little by little as the Lord began to deal with me in more personal & spiritual ways with discernment and divine direction that I never experienced in my entire life. The magnitude and level of my tears amazingly decreased within a short time. My life was being transitioned to a more spiritual realm that was unexplainable to man but yet understanding to God. The unexpected level of healing I experienced was derived from the strength of God and the prayers of the righteous. The triumph not only restored my hope but also restored my perspective in life.

MY BIRTHING SEASON:

As I reflect back many years ago, before my husband died, there were many times I had dreams of babies who were of different races and conditions. The babies were either given to me in the dreams or they were lost; and I would rescue them. These babies were found grieving, suffering due to lack of hope, and suffering without support. It was divinely both revealed and ministered to me that when you have dreams about babies, this is not necessarily a sign of natural pregnancy but a spiritual pregnancy that God himself was birthing on the inside of you. Several people had dreams of me being pregnant and not even realizing that these were signs of spiritual birth instead of natural birth. My encounters with these types of birth dreams occurred from 5 to 7 years. There were times that I woke up from the dreams, crying and praising the Lord. Little did I know these dreams prepared me for the most unknown and unexpected experiences in my life. These dreams being birthed within me would soon reach their delivery season.

Out of the many dreams I had, there was one particular dream I would like to share that stimulates the reason behind my purpose. This dream stood out from all of the rest, and I knew it resulted from all the pain I had suffered. In this dream, I held a baby in my arms while my late husband was standing behind me. This signified the push from him to let me know to go forth and do what I was purposed to do. The baby was wrapped in white clothing. I was dressed in a white suit. In the dream, there was also a white cloth found on my lap. As I was holding the baby, we were prepping ourselves to take a picture together. In the dream, we were all smiling. As I began to gather my thought processes, I realized that my late husband, who was behind me, was pushing me to be bold and step out with the purpose & ministry that God has given to me.

A RESULT FROM MY BIRTHING SEASON:

As a result of the dreams I encountered, I could not just push and deliver what was inside of me. I found myself helping others deliver what was growing inside of them by sharing their story to help others. The umbilical cord that was symbolically attached to me for so long was now becoming detached from me. The most devastating time of my life and the most significant pain I suffered helped to produce my purpose in life. It has allowed me to encourage all those who have suffered unexpected traumas and setbacks in their lives. You have something on the inside that is waiting to be birthed and experience its delivery season. Every pain you have faced leads you to deliver that gift, purpose, ministry, and business in your due season. You have to realize every pain, every setback, every battle, every disappointment, and warfare you have faced in your life did not come to break you down FROM THE GOOD but to build you up FOR THE GREATER. That loved one you have lost, that spouse you have lost, that peace you feel like you have lost, that happiness that you feel like you have lost; just know that all of those elements are right there to help carry you through life's struggles. There may be times when you feel like you are at the end of life's rope but remember you have to reach beyond the break of the rope to get to the other side of blessings. You won't know how strong the other side of the rope is unless you get a grip, hold tight, and stretch to the other side. Remember that your greatness can be developed not just after the storm but also during the storm. Your storm did not come to destroy you but develop you, mold you, prepare you, and establish you for greatness. When there is lightning in a storm, it strikes something with much power and energy. Become empowered from the lightning in the storm, get up, rise, & live to do what you were created and uniquely designed to do.

MY PURPOSE BEHIND THE BIRTHING SEASON:

From my own personal divine revelations, it was defined what it was I was divinely called to do. My purpose was to help others heal from their brokenness, pain, and setbacks in their lives. After experiencing the ultimate spiritual pregnancy in July 2020, my purpose was revealed to me by the Lord. The purpose and vision were then birthed in January 2021. From my pain, a resource ministry was designed to provide different resources to those who have suffered the loss of their loved ones. The name of this ministry is **W.O.W. Winning Over Warfare Resource Ministries, LLC.** This ministry includes mental & emotional health support, grief support, financial assistance resources, weekly inspirations, and other types. The ministry also supports those suffering from unexpected traumas in their lives and feels like all hope is lost. It helps push those that are weak and feel like giving up. It is designed to nourish the weary who require resources to help them win from their personal warfare. It also includes enabling others who have suffered hurt to help share their stories and testimonies to others. It is time to walk in your own calling and fulfill that purpose that you are designed to do. The world is waiting for your gift to be revealed from your pain and boldness to be brought to life from your storm. No matter the level of the pain, you can recover, reset, renew and restore yourself.

With God, you can live again and win over every battle. It is time to be purpose-driven and no longer a victim of depression & oppression. It is time to take the wheel to your destiny and allow these four gears to shift you to the next highway of your life and purpose (P. Peace; D. Direction; R. Revelation; and N. Newness).

P for Peace: Peace obtained can allow you to become better.

D for Direction: divinely Directed to go into the next dimension of your life without any distractions detouring you.

R for Revelation: if it has been Revealed to you what you are purposed to do. Tell your story to others who need to hear it and be delivered from their hurts.

N for Newness: when you have Newness in your mind, spirit, and heart, you can move on with your life yet cherish those memories of your loved ones.

CHAPTER

Beautifully Broken

Keisha Heard

Some things can break the human soul, break us down, shatter our hearts, self-image, and life itself comes crashing down. Life has now come to a complete stop. You have no idea what to do or even where to turn. All you know is your world has been completely ripped apart, and a piece of you has been taken from this world. A void has been formed and you have an emptiness that will never go away. Drugs won't fix it, alcohol won't fix it, and sex won't numb it. Not even church can't help it.......You never think things can happen to you, or you think you're too young for this or that until it happens. Well, take it from me; life can instantly change. but I have come to find out that there is beauty in darkness.

I was 20 when I met my soulmate, the man I thought I would spend the rest of my life with. He loved me past my flaws and all my insecurities. I remember him telling me two weeks into our relationship that I was going to be his wife. I laughed. At 20 years old, I was not thinking about getting married and didn't even think I ever would. But I fell madly in love with him. I like to call it *'agape love'*. In biblical terms, it's called unconditional love, or the highest form of love. We always said, *"No matter what, we would never leave each other. Till death do us part."* Who knew it would come so soon? I heard Td Jakes say one time, and I quote, *"The only reason we survive grief, the only reason we don't lose our minds, the only reason we don't cry until we die, is that one day, and you never know which day that is, you'll walk into restoration. It's not that you still don't love them or miss them, but all of a sudden, God restores your soul."* The loss of a spouse feels like the ripping away of two souls. To me, it's the worst kind of pain a person can experience. But again, in that dark place, I found beauty and myself.

My husband and I had a very rocky relationship from the get-go. However, I believed that every love was real. Regrettably, I can admit I was a victim of dysfunctional love, which could best be described as a trauma bond. A trauma bond can be defined as an emotional attachment between two people but develops out of hurt. It's a recurring cycle of love, lust, and pain. Two hurting people who just wanted to save each other. Our relationship was more like each other's diseases but treating each other like rehabs. About 6-7 months into the relationship, I discovered that my husband was a drunk. And being the person I was at the time, I dealt with anger issues and my own past trauma. So, you can imagine the interactions we had with each other. He would drink to cope with childhood issues and current home problems. My way of dealing with things was to fight and lash out. The marital collisions were not very good ones. But we hung in there because I loved him, and he loved me. We came from two different worlds, the south side of Chicago and Naperville, Illinois. Our families disagreed with us being together, but we didn't care. We were determined to stick things out. But in all the sticking together, I was slowly losing myself and had no idea who I was as a person. I was losing pieces of me I had not even found yet. I was losing the possibilities of discovering my full potential or identity. However, it's funny how the most hurtful times in your life can pivot you into the place you were initially meant to be. How it positions you to discover your greatest strengths and allows you to help others even in your own pain while at the same time healing yourself. God knows what to take away from us so that we go where He needs us to be. At the moment, it hurts, and it's devastating, but He does not allow things to happen to us for no reason. And when you look back, you understand why.

September 26, 2015 was the happiest day of my life. The day my husband and I decided to become one. It felt like we were the only ones in the room. Standing before God, and I was marrying the man of my dreams. It was the best day of my life and a turning point because often, we as women think that a title or marriage can save a relationship, but it doesn't. Who they are before the wedding day is who they'll be after. In my opinion, it gets worse because now you are tied to each other. Another thing I learned is that marriage is a full-time job, and it has its ups and downs, and people really don't understand what vows mean; the for-better-for-worse and till-death-do-us-part until they actually experience it. Shortly after my husband and I got married, we knew something was wrong. In my husband's words, we were trying to build a family and wanted to leave an empire and legacy. But after two miscarriages, we realized there was a severe problem. I discovered I had several issues. **PCOS (polycystic ovarian syndrome)** is a condition where the ovaries produce a lot of testosterones and make ovulation almost non-existent. I also discovered I had a condition called **adenomyosis**. It is a condition where the endometrial tissue grows abnormally into the uterine wall and causes irregular and prolonged bleeding, making it almost impossible to stay pregnant without miscarrying. After two losses, we never really recovered from those. We just picked up the pieces we could and kept moving towards the goal. But when proper healing is not done, and issues are covered up, it creates more problems. Healing is so important because if we had actually addressed the loss of those babies, we probably would have seen that we weren't ready; but instead, we went through four more years of failed fertility treatments. Time and money spent, all for nothing. That's how I felt at the time. I didn't even know God was keeping me from so many things. I only saw what was in front of me at that time. I wanted a family, and this was my husband, and God would bless us with a child. Everything happens in His timing and according to His will. You don't see the why until later on.

March 29, 2019, changed my life forever. It was a normal day. We were moving into the final phases of IVF. My husband was so happy. He just kept saying all day, *"I can't believe I am about to be a father. Our time is finally here."* The last words he said to me were, *"okay, baby, see you when I get home."* To this day, I am thankful to God that He allowed my husband to make it all the way home to me. I went into a deep sleep that night, and I woke up to a feeling that something was wrong or just off. I immediately texted my husband, *"where are you?"* No reply came. I lay back down and still couldn't shake off the feeling. I looked outside and saw his car parked behind mine. It was raining. I noticed his emergency lights on. I put on my clothes and ran outside. My neighbors were standing at his car door and asked, *"Isn't this your husband?"* I said, *"yes"* and walked up to see him slumped over in the passenger seat. I began to shake him, saying, *"baby wake up, get up!"* But again, no response. I proceeded to cup my hands around his face, and I just remembered him looking at me with this blank stare. No eye movement at all. I immediately panicked. My neighbor attempted CPR, and 911 was there in less than five minutes. The paramedics began working on him, and we got him to the hospital. I prayed the whole way to the hospital, but deep down, I already knew. When we got to the hospital, I walked to the back of the ambulance, and they pulled him out, and I just knew. He had the same blank stare as he wasn't even here. But even in that, my mind had not completely comprehended what was going on. I asked my family and my Pastor to accompany me to the chapel of the hospital. I went to the alter and just screamed, *"God, just please do not take my husband. Whatever we need to do as a couple, I will make sure we will do it. Whatever he needs to do as a man, I will make sure he does it, but please don't take him from me. We will fix it."* The worst feeling in the world is when you beg God for something, and then he doesn't do it, or you think this is the plan He had for your life, but then you find out it's not. The moment I was told my husband left this world; time stopped. My worst fears had come true. The next thing I knew was I was kissing his forehead before the coroner took him away.

Now what? God? Why? Why me? Why him? All these questions came that night and constantly over the past two years. Every time, I would see a friend pregnant or see someone get married. I would ask, *why me? Why did my life have to stop? Why does my journey have to be different?* These weren't the plans we had, but God's plans are never our plans. I had to figure out how to trust God and navigate through the highs and lows of grief and being a young widow. It took a lot of therapy and facing the truth about what my former life and marriage were. I had to deal with things that I had hidden over the years. I had to finally understand what addiction was and how it affected my family and my marriage. I had to be honest with myself on why I even stayed in my marriage as long as I did and come to terms with some of my own personal demons I was fighting. It was some hard truths I had to face, but to be healed and help people, I had to go through the process, and the process was hard and painful. I quit a few times, and then I restarted. I quit a few more times and then tried again, but I made it. Who would have ever thought the most painful and devastating experience would have birthed the woman I am today?

I began to discover myself. My transformation was like a butterfly out of her cocoon. I birthed so many gifts that made me able to help other women and be compassionate towards them. I developed the gift of discernment that allowed me to become aware or sense when other people are hurting. I am able to read between the lines and hear them through the pain without them even going into too many details. I developed the art of sensitivity and being able to relate with others. I had to allow myself to feel every emotion, even those I didn't want to feel. Feeling those emotions allowed me to connect with other women and be a go-to for them in time of need. I have been featured on a podcast about being widowed. I was featured on the *A Fly* widow podcast by Dr. Alisha Reed. The title of my segment was *'You're too young to be a widow'* (episode 8). I have been able to speak on different platforms and told my story on how I have navigated through widowhood, found a new identity, and how I have found that the best love is self-love. I also spoke on my very own mentor Kimberly Nicole Johnson, Wednesday's segment called *'On the couch with Kimberly.'* I spoke about my story, how I became a widow and how I have navigated through the past two years.

I heard this quote by one of my favorite Pastors, T.D. Jakes. *"The tougher the day, the greater the strength."* The strength that has come out of me being a widow has been phenomenal. You never know what you can handle or how strong you are until you are put in that situation. I have found a new me, and in return, I will use that new superpower to help others. For so long, my identity was tied to who my husband was and what he liked and disliked, and I completely lost myself in marriage and wanting to become a mother. These last two years, I have rediscovered myself and found my divine purpose. I often wonder why God chooses pain to get our attention, and I have to conclude that He knows what to take away to get us where we need to be. The most painful and devastating moments will lead us to where God needs us to be. My husband was like an idol to me, and the word tells us to have no other Gods before Him. He was my crutch. He was my everything. I probably would never have accomplished the things I have accomplished if he was still here. I wouldn't be the woman I am today if God hadn't shaken some things up. The blinders were taken off my eyes, and I began to see life differently. I could never go back to my old life, nor could I go back to the person I used to be. I do miss and still love my husband, but I would not want to go back to my old life. God does things for a reason and in his own timing and seasons, and we don't understand them at the moment, but we understand them by and by. We then look back and see why the journey was the way it was, and we become someone else's survival guide. Someone else will lose their spouse and have all the same questions; they will feel like they can't make it and like the pain will never end, and then that's when I will step in and say, "let me help you."

> *The Spirit of the Sovereign Lord is on me because the Lord has anointed me to proclaim good news to the poor. He has sent me to bind up the brokenhearted, to proclaim freedom for the captives and release from darkness for the prisoners, to proclaim the year of the Lord's favor and the day of vengeance of our God, to comfort all who mourn, and provide for those who grieve in Zion; to bestow on them a crown of beauty instead of ashes, the oil of joy instead of mourning, and a garment of praise instead of a spirit of despair.*
> **-Isaiah 61 1-3**

CHAPTER

Covid Didn't Break Me

Dr. Sandra McGowan-Watts

March 17, 2020, started off like any other day. It was the beginning of what we thought would be a two-week lockdown. Little did I know it would become an extended quarantine, which seemed like an eternity, a change in my current way of life, and the trajectory of my future was approaching. This particular day, Steve, Justise, and I took a day road trip to southern Illinois, so I could complete a work assignment. Two days prior, we had just celebrated Steve's 51st birthday. Usually, Steve and I would go to dinner alone, but this year was different. The girls went to dinner with us. We laughed and joked about this being the last day to sit down for dinner in a restaurant because the lockdown was starting. We joked about how it would be a long two weeks, and we were going to have a hard time because we loved to eat in restaurants. We were the ultimate foodies. Steve was the one who invited the girls, and I'm so glad he did. We had a wonderful dinner.

Back to March 17th. That day was beautiful. It was our first road trip with just the three of us: Steve, Justise, and I. Little did I know, this would be our last trip. We laughed and joked. Steve and Justise kept cracking jokes. We were a family, and we were happy. I was happy, he was happy, and Justise had her mommy and daddy together on a trip. Never in a million years would I have thought that our lives would be turned upside down four weeks later. Never could I have fathomed the life I once had, and the dreams I had would be gone. Little by little, every fragment of my life would disappear. Who would have ever thought a little bug, a virus, would wreak havoc on this world and change who I am forever? Over the next few weeks, COVID-19 began to attack the body of the man I love. My strong yet gentle, husband was being attacked.

The nightmare began on April 2, 2020, when my mother-in-law fell ill, and my husband went to check on her. After getting her to the hospital, we received a call the next day, advising she had COVID and needed to be intubated. That was a Friday. Later that evening, my husband became ill. He stayed in bed all day Saturday. Oddly enough, Sunday was Palm Sunday. Steve felt somewhat good and came to the kitchen to eat with us. We were having virtual church service and having communion. He partook in the ritual with us. This was strange but good. Steve was not one to go to church but yet he was a man of God.

Monday, he felt more ill, and over the week, he became weaker and weaker. I remember him waking me Good Friday morning because he was writhing with fever and chills. I gave him medicine and prayed over my husband, asking God to heal his body. I anointed his head with oil, believing my faith would heal him. Later that morning, I took him to be tested for COVID, and his vital signs were stable. We were told the results would be back later that week. I went to work later that afternoon, calling home every chance I got to make sure he was okay; at that time, he said he was. But deep down, I think he was scared and did not want to alarm the girls or me. He was too strong of a man to have us worrying. One day during this week, I remember him yelling at me to leave him alone and get out of the room with him because we both could not be ill because there would be no one to take care of her (meaning Justise, our 12-year-old).

As the weekend progressed, I watched him get sicker and sicker. He became weak to the point where I had to take him to the hospital. I remember us arguing because he did not want to go, but finally, after I took a long walk and came back home, he asked me to take him to the ER. He was too weak to even bathe or dress alone, so I had to do it. Something I know he hated, but I did it with no questions because I love him. That was April 12, 2020, Easter Sunday, the last day I physically saw my husband. The last thing he told the girls before we left was, I will be back. As I drove to the hospital, I could see the fear in his face. At one moment, he told me that God told him he would be alright. I could see his body getting weaker and weaker. He was no longer this strong man, but someone who was fighting with all he had to breathe. When I left him, he was only concerned about me getting home safe. But that was Steve, always concerned about others.

For the next few weeks, COVID -19 attacked his organs, and they began to fail. There were sleepless nights and days of my children forcing me to eat. Every day was the same:

- Wake up.
- Get ready for work.
- Call the hospital to check on him.
- Go to work.
- Come home.
- Call the hospital to check on him again and go to bed.

Most days, there were calls from the doctors updating me or asking for consent to do a procedure. As the days went on, he became sicker, and I had to make some hard choices about his care. Decisions no 46-year-old wife should have to make.

May 8, 2020, at 3:56pm, my life changed. I remember getting a call from his nurse. I remember the sound of her voice telling me that he had died. Before receiving that call, we smelled smoke in our house. We could not figure out where it was coming from, so we called the fire department. They walked all throughout the house and could not find a source. After receiving the call, I realized it was my Steve. Smoking his last cigar in our home. Testing me to see if I knew what to do if I smelled smoke. I passed the test. He could not rest in the arms of God and with his loved ones who had passed on before, including his mom (who also died from COVID one week prior) until, he was sure. He promised the girls he would be back, and he did come back, just not the way we wanted.

Looking back, I now know I made the right decisions about his care. I would not change one thing. Every procedure I agreed to, even though I knew it may not save him, I would have them perform again. Many times, I knew he would not have wanted certain things done, but I chose to anyway. I had to give my young husband a fighting chance. He was only 51. He had so much more life left to live. So many plans left to live out. I wanted more for him, but God saw differently. It was during that period of Steve being sick and hospitalized I realized what love really means. I learned what my marriage vows really meant. Steve and I lived our vows until the day he died. We lived for better or worse, richer or poorer, sickness and in health until death did us part.

During Steve's illness and even since his death, I have felt every emotion imaginable, but mostly I feel sadness and guilt. Sad that I was not able to be there when he needed me most. The country was on lockdown, and hospitals were closed to visitors. I begged several times to visit, to just hold his hand, but I was told no. All I was able to do was see him via video chat. For me, that was no way to watch the man I love live his last days. I wonder if he knew how much I loved him and how hard I was fighting for him.

Guilt... *did I bring this virus home? How could the doctor not save the person she loves? Should I have taken him to the hospital sooner?* It has been challenging living with this guilt. As a physician, the last thing you ever want to do is make your loved ones ill. I feared I would get sick and bring the virus home from the beginning of this public health crisis. I also felt survivor's guilt. *Why did I not get sick? Why did I not have to be hospitalized? Why did I survive? Why was I left to live this life without him? Why was I left to raise our daughter alone?* I never imagined being a solo parent. Why was I left to have to explain to a 12-year-old why her daddy died and why she would not have the privilege to have the first man she loved here to see her graduate, go off to college, walk her down the aisle. All these unanswered questions and no answers. I will never get answers to these questions, but I have to trust God and trust the process. I have to remember God has a plan for my pain. One day, He will show me why I had to endure this ordeal.

So, you may wonder, why do I keep going, what keeps me going? When I look into my daughter's eyes, who looks just like her daddy, I realize I cannot give up. I cannot stop. She is my motivation. Whenever I feel down or feel like I cannot make it, I look into those big, beautiful eyes and remember that life continues. There is a future for me. There is a future for her. This child is the spitting image of her dad, from his looks to his behavior. She keeps me on my toes, as he did. She has ambitions and dreams that I need to help keep her on track to accomplish. She loves to cook, something her dad took pride in. She wants to one day have her own bakery, something he always dreamed of. His legacy is continuing through her, and I need to keep her on track. So, I have to stay strong and focused on getting her there.

The other reason I keep going is to keep my medical practice open and thriving. We all have a ministry in life, and practicing medicine is what I know God wants me to do. January 2019, I opened my own medical practice, and my husband was my biggest supporter. He spent countless hours and sleepless nights helping me make my dreams a reality and become who I am. He worked hard to allow me to become great and make our business successful. My business became his business. My dream became his dream. Steve put his career to the side to help build my practice, which became our practice. So, I cannot give up now. When I want to give up, I can hear him saying, woman up, you can do it. This is my motivation, to make sure Steve's life and living were not in vain.

What I have learned on this journey is you will not completely understand until you walk this path. Some days, you feel you can conquer the world. Other days, you lay around in bed all day wondering why. *Why you and why this path.*

This is also a lonely journey. It's nothing worse than sitting in a room full of people and still feeling alone. Even if you have a village present, you still feel alone without your spouse by your side sharing your life. Through this journey, you also learn who is there for you. I have learned that friends and family are not there like you expect.

Often, it is because life goes on for them, and they do not understand. They do not know what you are feeling. They also do not know what to say. What do you say to a 46-year-old widow? I have learned to lean into the ones who are there and not be angry with those we really do not understand how to be there or what I really need. I have also learned to accept help from others and ask for what I need. I have learned that most people in my village are here for me. Steve left a legacy; his life goes on. It goes on through his girls and me.

I am not only living, but I'm thriving. I have kept my business afloat despite grief and a pandemic. I'm learning to channel my grief into helping others. I have been afforded the opportunity to speak about my experience. I have found joy in helping others. Although I have questioned God on many occasions and been angry with God, wondering why me, I realize He still has a plan for me. God has His hands on me, and He has greatness in store. I just need to heed to His word and listen to Him.

I am also finding who I am. I am learning what I like and do not like. I have also picked up new hobbies and am enjoying them. I say, "*if 2020 did not teach me anything else, it taught me to enjoy life because tomorrow is not promised.*" I have learned to live my life and have fun doing it. Traveling is the one thing I'm beginning to love. Traveling is something we always wanted to do but never found the time. As I have gone through my year of firsts, I have traveled three times during a pandemic. As I am finishing this piece, I am traveling to Puerto Rico to celebrate my 47th birthday. It is bittersweet not having him physically here, but I feel his spirit. I know he is happy with the woman I have become. I am not letting my grief stop me from celebrating and living my life.

What's next for me? **Speaking**. Telling my story to help others, so someone can see that you can survive and make it when adversities come into their life. It is my dream to continue to minister to others about the great things they can do when they put all their trust in God. What I have learned is when you are at the bottom, God will pick you up and place you in a position to minister to others. I will continue to do this as long as I am breathing.

To the widow out there who thinks she cannot make it, trust me, you can. When depression, anxiety, and/or fear start to sink in, go to the word of God. Read the word, meditate on the scripture, Jeremiah 29:11: ***"For I know the plans I have for you declares the Lord, plans to prosper you and not harm you, plans to give you hope and a future."*** Trust me, there is a plan for your life. God will give you the strength, courage, and endurance to get through. Remember, the race is not always given to the strong, but those who can endure and persevere.

God can and will get you through this trial, and you will come out victoriously. I know it may be challenging, and right now, you cannot see it, but there is a purpose to your pain, and if you lean unto God's word, He will direct your path.

Remember, it's okay to not be okay. It's okay to be angry and mad and ask God why. But also remember to be open to God's answer. There is nothing wrong with seeking counseling and talking to others. I recommend you seek wise counseling from someone who is experienced in grief counseling. Someone who will give unbiased advice. Counseling saved me. It is because of counseling; I can keep going and move forward. I also say, never be afraid to ask for and accept help when it is offered. You are not in this alone, and many are ready, willing, and able to help you on this journey.

On May 8, 2020, I did not see how I would make it, but I did. I did not think there would be a light at the end of the tunnel, but it is. I did not think I would smile again, but with God's grace, I am. And not only am I surviving, but I am also thriving, and I know I will continue to soar because God is on my side. This life is not just my life, it is our life (Steve and mine), and with God's grace, I will continue to move forward and live victoriously.

CHAPTER

My Wonderful Life

Dr. Debra Pope-Johnson

My husband Frank shielded me from the worries of life for over 30 years. When I first met him, I remember he was the most mature man I had ever met. I had traveled to Albany, GA, with his cousin for the New Year's Celebration of 1982. He came over to his aunt's house where we were staying to greet his cousin and stated he would take us out that evening for the New Year's Eve celebration. I dressed for the evening and went along, not really paying any attention to him. By the time we got to the club, we were constantly talking, and he had my full attention. He was serious and driven, a gentleman, single and unencumbered, precisely what I needed (God sent). He even agreed to drive us back home to Tallahassee the next day. It was love at first sight. He and I were connected.

On New Year's Eve, he gave me his last name. He always addressed me as Debra P. Johnson from 1/1/82 until the day he died 4/21/12. We were married on 4/26/82. We would have been married for 30 years had he lived five more days. We have two daughters Tolaison and Ashley, and two granddaughters Elle and Olivia. He loved children, pets, and most of all, he loved me. Through all of the ugly and pretty of life, he stayed, we stayed, we remained us. I have never experienced a stronger love than which existed between Frank and myself. Frank was a man of few words, but I knew absolutely he was committed to us, we, and family.

Frank passed suddenly, but we knew something was wrong because he fell twice the Thursday prior when trying to enter our home, after sitting in his truck for over 2 hours, after arriving home from dialysis. My youngest daughter and I helped him up, and I wanted him to stay in the house and sleep in the bedroom, but he refused and went back outside to his office. My oldest daughter had just gotten married on December 30, 2011, and this was going to be her first trip home with her husband to attend the wedding of one of her bridesmaids. Tolaison arrived early in the a.m. and helped him back out to his office with the aid of a pair of crutches I had in the house. That Friday, I called him four times (each time asking him to call the doctor), but we never saw him. My son-in-law took his dinner to his office. He was scheduled for dialysis at 10:30 on Saturday, April 21, 2012, at 9:30 a.m. I told everyone seated around the breakfast table that someone needed to go out and wake Frank so he wouldn't be late for his dialysis appointment. After a round-robin of *"enee minee miny mo,"* my son-in-law was chosen. He was taking way too long to return to the table, so I sent my younger daughter out to see what was taking them so long. She came tripping and stumbling back, yelling for us to call 9-1-1. I immediately went out to the office and found my son-in-law attempting to get my husband flat on the floor for CPR. I was standing there with the 9-1-1 dispatcher who was telling me to administer CPR, and I couldn't move. The ambulance arrived, and I was told to go put on clothes to ride in the ambulance with him to the hospital. I remember clear as day me asking God to please let him live, and I just kept repeating, *"No Not Frank, Please No Not Frank."*

God _knows_ about your situation. But with _every_ test and _every_ trial, _there_ is revelation that God is able to _supply_ every one of your needs. He's here to _touch_ you, heal you, He'll set you free. ~ Darryl Coley ~ song *"Broken but I Am Healed."*

I couldn't talk about Frank's death. I closed my mind and compartmentalized my heart. In my mind, he was ever-present. I lived in the sad world of my mind. My heart was broken, and I was irrevocably shattered. One morning about a month after Frank died, one of my coworkers called me and asked if I knew I still had a job? I said I knew I had a job, and she wanted to know when I was planning to return to work? I had this thing about fixing my face when confronted about anything negative or hurtful, and I did not know how to face my coworkers and teachers with grief, hurt, loneliness, and my shattered existence showing all over me. I gave her a date a week away so I could *"get myself together."* The day before I returned to work, I asked my secretary to send out an email stating I did not want to discuss my husband's death in any way with people. I said I was in mourning, and to constantly discuss it would take too much of a toll on my ability to move forward on a day-to-day basis with my life.

I needed to work. Although I had insurance money, everything thing else was tied up because I was too young (54) to collect anything but half of what my husband would have received as a pension. I was now responsible for all the bills of the household. Previously Frank paid all the household bills, and I played with my money. He had set up all the bills to be paid automatically from our "joint" account in which he deposited his paycheck weekly. But no more deposits were coming from his paychecks, and now I was responsible for all bills with one-fourth of what he would have usually been paid. I still did not wake up. My oldest daughter tried to make sense of this financially, and I just spun my wheels at work, came home, and went to bed. I did not go anywhere and had no desire to re-engage with my previous life.

MOVING GRIEF FROM MY BRAIN TO MY HEART

It took four years for me to open the cards and letters I received from the funeral. I had a DVD that they played at the wake I still have not viewed. I went through the cards and things, and even though I ordered printed thank you cards, they were never sent. I just could not. What triggered me to open the cards, and such was when my father died (September 2016) and the birth of my granddaughter (April 2016). I went to Denver and handled the work of my father's death, and to New York to witness the birth of my granddaughter. Although I was not really close to my father; witnessing the birth of my granddaughter gave me hope to continue to live. I began to think about Frank and his fatherly role to his daughters and his role as a husband. Please notice I said *think*. My grief had never moved from my head. All my life, I have "overthought" most things. I was finally ready to address Frank's presence in the life of others and their care for me now that he had died. It was time to feel with my heart.

> **I used several methods to cope. Find what's best for you.**

I have been a member of Facebook since 2010. I see it as a positive way to deal with life and communicate with people I value. When I lost my husband, it is where I posted information about his service, where I thank and remember him each Father's Day and the day of his birth; and where I post my growth, or lack thereof, each year on his death day and our anniversary. I joined several grief groups, and I am currently an administrator of a group of Healing Hearts. When I moved from membership to becoming an administrator of a grief group, it changed my understanding of growth and healing.

It helped me identify raw grief, fear, loneliness, depression and motivated me to pursue healing. I met the widow who had the vision for this anthology in the Black Widow Women Empowered group as a mentor. We women/men/widows/widowers as members of grief groups have such power. Possibly because of the collaborative nature of these groups. We are hurt, so we want someone to help us understand and benefit from the knowledge of how we worked through. I have received some real answers to that part of myself that was in turmoil. In exchange, I have given what I thought was needed loving and sincere *advice to others.*

SURVIVAL AFTER LOSS

> *"You survived what you thought would break you.*
> *Now straighten that crown and move forward like the Queen you are."*
> *-Unknown*

After his death, I dreamed of him sitting silently on the living room couch and me frantically trying to figure out how to give all the insurance money back. I had spent a large part of it on the funeral, paying off the house, doing some remodeling, and paying off his truck. In my dreams, he has only spoken to me once when I, in my infinite wisdom, decided I couldn't heal until I sold the house we had built and lived in for 30 years. He told me that the house wasn't just for me but for the family, and to get rid of it would be risking our stability as a family. Nevertheless, I still have the house.

I had always thought life was fair, and once you took a loss as great as your husband, you really should not have to suffer any more for a long time. Boy, was I wrong? Life is a challenge, and things are going to come to disrupt your existence. But God.... God can carry you when you can't walk. Because of God, I have Hope and Praise. He will do just what he promised and will *"see you through."*

THE LOSS OF PEOPLE YOU THOUGHT WERE YOUR FRIENDS

> *"Where did everyone go? One by one, they disappeared.*
> *Maybe they didn't want to see me, feel my pain, or deal with my grief.*
>
> **-Gary Roe**

On this journey, I have grieved the loss of friends who stopped communicating with me. One of my husband's friends said he wouldn't be around much because of his wife. When I asked why he said I was too attractive of a widow to be around married men. I had been friendly with this man my entire marriage and had not had any reason to be suspect of wanting anything from him except friendship. I saw him years later, and he stated I had been constantly on his mind, and he was sorry for the way he had acted after my husband died. This man worked with my husband for over thirty years and lived in my neighborhood. I tried going out with single ladies, which was not a fit because they were wholly independent. My life made me very dependent on my husband, and some of the single ladies I met had contempt for married women and men. The couples we would infrequently interact with did not call. In the absence of this, I worked with the friends and family I had left. They listened, laughed, and many thought I had lost my mind sometimes, but they stayed, and I will always treasure their friendship.

GRIEVING IS PERSONAL

> *"Healing comes in waves, and maybe today the waves hit the rocks, and that's okay, that's okay darling. You are still healing. You are still Healing".*
>
> *-Ijeoma Umebinyuo*

For a long time after Frank died, I would compare my experience with others who had suffered a loss. I would look for and compare the magnitude of my loss with others who shared their experiences. *Oh, their husband was old… Oh, their husband had a lengthy illness… Oh, their husband committed suicide…Oh, they do not have to work… Oh, they did not have insurance*, and on and on, I would go. Over time, I finally understood that grief is personal, and it was impossible to feel the magnitude of the loss someone was experiencing. I have whispered many a prayer for fellow widows. Their experiences are just as hurtful to them as mine was and hard to overcome without help. I read voraciously and would take this same attitude to stories written by and for widows until I finally understood that healing would take a mosaic of experiences. What was painful for me might not be as painful for another widow(er). It was vital for me to read and identify what I might need for help and leave the rest of the story for someone else. Without judgment! Without trying to make it fit my circumstances!

HEALING TAKES TIME

> *"Right now, when your loss is so fresh, it may be difficult for you to imagine that this pain will ever go away. But in time, the Blessing of God's unfailing grace will soften the hurt that you are feeling and bring your heart the peace, comfort, and hope it needs to heal."*
>
> *-Unknown*

The main thing we need to believe is that time is a commodity. I grieve those widows who refuse to realize God still has a purpose for their life. You are here for a reason – a purpose. I have a different relationship with God. I grew to understand that God has carried me a lot longer than the 30 years I was married to Frank. I had to lean on him because I felt I was in the middle of a tornado. He held my hand in the midst of it all. Yolanda Adams sings a song where she states, *"this didn't catch him by surprise,"* and initially, I was acting like God, who is all-knowing, did not know about this.

My mother died when I was 18 months old. I grew up without a mother. It was not until I was sent to live with my grandmother that I knew what a mother's love was like. She died when I was twelve, and I never called anyone else mama. Everyone kept their identifiers, aunt, stepmother, uncle, cousin, etc., because they could and would fail to fulfill a commitment to me and my life as a motherless child. I said all of this to say, *"without God, I could not have made it."* He is already there in anything that breaks your heart. He carries you and strengthens you to do his work. He gets your attention as you tend to what He has purposed for your life. I would always question him about my *purpose*. The answer is in the daily walk; be present, be loving, be kind, be mindful, be prayerful, and know that God has it in control.

SAYING GOODBYE

"Good-Bye can sometimes be the saddest word that we must say because it seems so final whenever loved ones pass away. But looking back in memory, we're comforted to know that love has never left us and will never let us go. And even though we cannot know exactly where or when we say goodbye believing we will surely meet again."

-Unknown

CHAPTER

Life Without Him

Pamela Cheatom

I didn't know October 30, 2019, about 6:30 am would be the last time I would ever see or speak with my husband. We kissed each other goodbye and said I love you as was usual. We talked multiple times throughout the day. Later in the day, I became alarmed because my husband only worked ten minutes away from home and had not come at his normal scheduled time. In my heart, I knew that something was wrong. I jumped into my car and followed the route that he would take to come home. Once I got to his job and saw his car, I knew something was very wrong. When I got inside, his personal belongings and keys to his car were sitting on a desk. I started calling his name over and over again, but there was no response. There were no other employees around. Something told me to go into the bathroom. Somehow, I got the bathroom door unlocked, and there, my husband lay unresponsive. All I saw was his legs under the bathroom stall. I immediately called 911. What took minutes seemed like an eternity. When the Fire Department got there, the captain came to me and said, *"We are so sorry there is nothing we can do; he is gone."*

At that moment of hearing, *"he's gone,"* I don't know how I felt; I was in shock. I didn't want to believe my husband was gone. The most difficult part of this was standing over my husband's lifeless body. However, an even more daunting task was telling my children that their dad was no longer here. Although they are grown, telling them was still very hard because I could not process it myself. So, how could I tell them he was gone. The first night without him, I cried the whole night inconsolably. *Whyyyyy?* I thought having faith in God was enough, even when my husband lay dead. I thought this could not be. This cannot be my new normal. We did not get to enjoy all the things we planned together. This was my soulmate; how could this be happening to me? I remember the morning he died; I had laid my hands on him and prayed for him before he went off to work. *"Was my prayer to God not enough? Did I not pray the right prayer? Did God not hear me that day?"* So many questions were racing through my mind. I thought perhaps I did not have enough faith in God, or he would still be here. Why did the Lord allow this person and that person to live but not my husband? Did I offend God and, as a result, would not allow my husband to live? Was it that I was not a good wife that could not get a prayer through concerning her husband to God? Did I not pray enough for him? Why didn't I have more time with my husband? He loved me for me. He was my best friend, lover, boyfriend, and husband. He was my provider, protector, priest of the home, parent, and grandfather. Do I really have to go through the rest of my life without him? I often told the Lord, *"God, you are just and sovereign, but this is not fair."*

When he passed away, I had nothing to give to anyone. I felt lost. The first year was the most brutal because it was new, and I had to do it alone. For the first six months, I really hibernated. I was cautious who I let get close and personal. This was intentional because people meant well but said a lot of unnecessary stuff. I don't think it was with malicious intent on their part. But how could they respond correctly to something they knew nothing about. I was not suicidal, but there were times I wanted to die. I did not want to experience the pain and the sorrow I was experiencing. Then it came to me; you cannot stay here in this dark place. My youngest daughter inspired me while I was in my dark place, and I think about that often. He did not get to see her graduate High School; he passed away before she walked the stage, approximately three weeks before graduation.

At first, my daughter did not want to walk across the stage because her dad would not be present. But then she decided she would walk the stage to honor him. My baby girl showed so much strength while her world was falling apart. She walked across the stage with grace, elegance, and a smile on her face. That's when I realized, *"If your baby girl can do this, then you can do it."*

On this journey, I have realized several things. I realized some of my questions, or maybe all, would not be answered. It was a divine operation, and the Lord was not going to reveal the WHY to me. I can't focus on the WHY because it will not bring him back. I realize I don't have to be an actress. There is a term I have heard so many times; *"sometimes you have to fake it until you make it."* But I continue to say to myself, *"I will not fake it until I make it."* This experience has been too painful to allow me to fake what I'm feeling. I began to pray and ask God to help me. The bible says in Psalms 147:3, *"He health the broken in heart, and bindeth their wounds."* That means the Lord can bandage up the wounds of my heart. So, I allow myself to feel whatever it is I am feeling. There were many days when I was irritable, angry, and sad. I also did not allow a label called depression to be placed on me. I was not depressed; I was grieving. I knew I would have to fight for my healing. I must choose again to live and not die. I began to do a lot of walking so I could meditate. On many of my walks, I was talking to God. I relieve a lot of stress when I walk. I allow myself to cry, especially during my hour commute to work. That's when I would get it all out of my system. I sought counseling to get assistance with processing my feelings. I also had a small group of friends that I trusted enough to say how I really felt.

I realized that my husband's passing had nothing to do with me. People are born, and there is an expiration date. We never know what we will go through in this walk called life. I learned, and I'm still learning to be grateful for the good days. I've also learned that there is something that can be gained from tragic life experiences. Although my husband is not here, life did not cheat him. We had so many beautiful memories that I was able to look back and just smile about. While he was here, he did everything to put a smile on my face and make me happy. We should enjoy the time we have with the people we love and appreciate the precious gems and gifts they are while they are with us. Because once they are gone, there is nothing else we can say or do for them.

Who could have imagined that my pain would turn into purpose? Had this NOT happened, I would never have known the strength I possessed. My focus is on moving forward. I realized I am not exempt from the painful experiences in life. I learned that most of my WHY had absolutely nothing to do with me as his wife. He did not belong to me; he belonged to God. God did not take my husband to punish me. My husband was carrying me physically and spiritually. I have also realized I was comfortable hiding behind my husband. He provided financially and protected me from anybody harming me. Often, I would not go to God to seek answers; I would go to my husband. I stopped having my own personal relationship with God. There was a thing I was strong enough to do, but I did not know because I was hiding behind my husband being a wife. I was hiding behind my children being a mother. There was so much more that God wanted me to accomplish as an individual, as Pamela, a person aside from the many titles I thought was me. I realized I lost my identity as a person. *Who am I now that he is gone?* I know that choosing happiness, choosing to live again does not mean that I have forgotten him. I used to feel guilty for being happy because he was not here. But that is so far from the truth. I'm not moving on without him. Instead, I move forward in purpose and healing. I'm learning myself all over again. As a widow/single woman, I am moving forward with my husband's love. I will love him until my last breath; that will never change. I am moving forward with all of the precious memories I still have to share with my children and grandchildren.

Life is not over because my husband died. Life is still beautiful. There is still a lot of love around in my children, grandchildren, extended family friends. I have since had two additional grandbabies since my husband's passing. It's incredible to me the timing of my grandbabies. My husband died, but then new life came. My sweet little grandbaby came. I told my family, "She is a precious gift at the right time." She needed our love and attention; it was a welcome distraction from our grief. I am now passing on the love and care I wanted to shower on my late husband to others in my life. What will never die is the beautiful love and memories that we shared; that will be carried over into eternity.

I will live my best life unapologetically without explanation to anyone. I know I can never be happy again based upon how someone else feels about the remainder of my story and how it should be written. I will move forward in life the way I want to do it. If I want to find love again, that is ok. If I choose to remain single, that is ok. What I realized during this process is that in this new chapter, I am excited for what the future holds. I am going to live my best life with my family and friends. I will be traveling and going to places my husband and I talked about. I will celebrate the fact that even though my husband is not here, we had a beautiful marriage that was an example to our children and other couples around us. I will cherish how good he was to me.

This next chapter is all about discovering me as an individual aside from being a wife, mother, and grandmother. I'm no longer able to hide in the shadows of my husband. This has made me come out of my comfort zone. Now, I will be intentional about getting to know myself as an individual woman. I will be intentional about doing activities on my own learning and being ok with just me. I will not be afraid to say no to others if I don't want or feel like doing something. I have started doing short day trips on my own just to enjoy nature, taking walks on my own, sitting outside in the back yard, letting the sun hit my face, reading a book, or just quietly sitting. I have also decided to go back to school and finish up my master's degree program. It's some time I started, but putting my family first, I put it on the backburner. Now it is time for me to go back and finish what I started. I am determined to travel to some of the many destinations my husband and I talked about. One of those places will definitely have to be tropical. I have not decided on the location yet, but I am pretty sure it will be the Caribbean. I did not want to admit it at first, but I'm also confident that I will find love again. I'm excited about falling in love again and being capable of giving my heart again to my next. I have actually signed up on a couple of popular dating sites. It has been challenging due to a global pandemic but not impossible. It has also been challenging because I have not been on the dating scene for almost 20 years. Meeting new people and communicating with people I don't know also pulls me out of my comfort zone. But it has been building my confidence. Even though I have run into a couple frogs, I am learning more about who I am in the process. I have so much hope because what I get to rediscover in this next journey is… ME!

Whatever you do… don't quit! Your children need you. Your grandbabies need you. YOU need you. I know if I could ever have a conversation with my husband, he would say, *"I know you're hurting, but I want you to keep pressing, keep praying, and most of all, keep praising the Lord."* I can hear him saying it now. As I write this down, I can see a big smile on his face. My faith in God was tested, but I yet believe in God.

CHAPTER

Catapulted Into Widowhood

Khalilah Richardson

November 23, 2020 was the day I was catapulted into a foreign world I never imagined myself in. The day began as a usual workday. Shallah, my husband, was up early getting ready for work. He came upstairs to kiss me goodbye on my cheek. He kissed me on my cheek because I still had what he called *'dragon breath,'* you know, the time before you get a chance to make it into the bathroom and brush your teeth. We always said we loved each other before leaving one another, and that day I mustered the words *"Have a good day"* through my half-tired, just waking up mood. Shallah replied, *"I will."* Moments later, I heard muffled voices outside, which sounded like an argument. I recognized the voices. Then my heart dropped. I ran downstairs to open the door and saw my husband and ex-boyfriend on our front porch. My husband came into the house and said, *"He stabbed me!"*

I remember the shock instantly coming over my body. *"What!!"* As I raced upstairs to get my phone, I felt like I was watching someone else's life. There was no way in the world this was our life. Shallah and I lived a peaceful life. We never had explosive arguments. We had extensive talks with our children when they did something wrong. Shallah never reacted to any situation violently, yet he was violently attacked in front of our house. I remember listening and responding to the 911 operator while yelling to my husband to wake up. His body slumped over at our front door while I prayed he would recover from this. The ambulance seemed to take forever to get there. Through my yelling and trying to save my husband, I had not noticed my children standing on the stairs watching me until my son said he heard the ambulance coming. My daughter tried to move things out of the way so that the front door would open wider so my husband could lie flat like the 911 responder was telling me to do. It seemed as though the paramedics took too long to attend to my husband. In the movies and on television shows, they appeared to move a lot faster. The first paramedic felt for a pulse and told the other paramedics that there wasn't one. I kept thinking, *"She is wrong."*

In my mind, they were going to put him in the ambulance and shock his heart back. I had seen this in the movies and on television shows. I know this is how it works. The paramedics just needed to move faster, and they would be able to save him. Well, none of that happened. Detectives and police officers swarmed my house asking me a million of the same questions until they finally told me that my husband had passed. I remember yelling out *"No"* over and over. Through the tears, I kept telling myself it was not true. We were planning our first anniversary for next year and the rest of our lives as we grew old together. There was no way in the world we had finally found our perfect mate, and now it was all over in a matter of minutes. We were blending a family and planning our lives for when all the children left the house. I thought we had so much more time together. Our motto was *"happy spouse, happy house."* We did not place one over the other. It was a competition to see who could outdo the other by making the other spouse happy.

For months I tried to convince myself that Shallah was working late and going out early in the morning. I couldn't sleep unless I was exhausted. The incident kept playing in my head over and over. I felt like I was living in fear and all alone. A range of emotions would consume me daily. I was confused as to why Shallah did not survive the attack. We were at the beginning of building our future. We were in love with each other. Our communication was finally in a good space, and our children were prospering and enjoying the blended family. Every unfulfilling relationship we had before meeting each other felt necessary for us to be so appreciative of each other. I also felt angry. How could the unhappiness of someone else's life take away our happiness? Why couldn't my ex have just killed himself? Did Shallah fight hard enough to stay? What if I had gotten outside faster? I could have helped my husband. I was, and still am, in denial. There is no way this happened to me. There is no way I was ever involved with a person who could initiate such a heinous attack.

I still feel like Shallah will come home one day. Although my mind knows different things, my heart will not accept reality. Shallah always told me he always had me, and he was not a liar. He called me his *'Sweetness'* because I was the sweetest thing that ever happened to him. There is no way he was taken from me so soon when we were beginning our forever. I was sad a lot while smiling for the public daily. I am a teacher, and I had to put on a good face for my students. That *"good face"* also had to be put on for my children, who constantly watched me, family, and friends who frequently checked in on me and expressed their condolences. That *"good face"* would break down every night when the world became quiet, and my thoughts became louder. The sadness would consume me with tears that people kept telling me would bring joy in the morning. That joy never came in the morning because my husband never returned to me in the morning. I found myself in a fog. I was drifting through the day, almost like an out-of-body experience. I would fall asleep through exhaustion but wake up an hour or two later, trying to escape my racing mind. This process lasted for months.

I have never been the type of person to stay unhappy for long. I longed to be "normal" again. I knew I had to get myself together. If not for me, then definitely for my children. They relied heavily on me, and I had to remember that I was a wife and a mother. I found a shirt that smelled like my husband's and laid it across a pillow. I placed it the long way on the bed next to me to pretend he was there as I slept. I continued to move through life in a fog for several more weeks. I still had children to comfort and raise. I still had a job to go to so I could continue to pay bills. I still had people that loved and cared for me that wanted to ease my pain. As much as I understood everything I had to do, I did not want to do it. I had to mentally psych myself up every day to move through this new foggy world.

I sought out a therapist because that is what everyone kept telling me to do. That session was one and done. She did not say anything to comfort me or give me any tools to maneuver through this painful process. I could tell that she meant well, and she tried to relate to my grief. Still, through her eyes and responses, I could also tell that my situation was something she had never encountered, and I could not waste my energy by continuing to see her while she tried to figure it out. In my mind, no one could help me with my grief. My husband was no longer coming back home, and there was not enough talking in the world to make me feel better.

Then I decided to go to a psychic medium because the only person who could give me comfort was my husband. Shallah was the only person I wanted to speak to and hear from. The first thing the psychic medium said to me made me burst out into tears because my husband had said something that we had only spoken about in private. The whole session was a crying session because I knew it was my husband talking to me. He told me his life ended at the highest he could have imagined, and he would not have changed anything. He would never stop loving me, and he knew I loved him. I left the session feeling a little better and setting my mind on doing what my husband had told me to do. He told me I had to get myself together for the children, and there was not another person to do it but me. I knew he was right because I could feel my children watching me and wondering how to navigate this tragedy.

After visiting the psychic medium, I felt like other things just started falling into place. A friend of my husband reached out to me and suggested an elder for me to speak to. He was the same elder my husband had frequented when he was alive for advice and clarity on different things that occurred throughout his life. I decided to reach out to the elder and learned that he was recently widowed. He suggested I write a few affirmations and repeat them daily. I wrote three affirmations for my grief and three affirmations for my trauma. They were written on sticky notes and placed on a board in my room. I wanted to see them when I needed and keep them away from anyone, I did not want to see them. These affirmations were only for me and my healing. I was amazed by the power of my mind by just repeating my affirmations. By creating my affirmations and not looking up random declarations online, I quickly memorized them, and they felt more personal in my grief journey. I had to continuously repeat them throughout the day for weeks before I noticed any change.

I also decided to dedicate one day a week to my husband. I chose Sunday because that was his only consistent day off. Every Sunday, I would unplug from the world and do something dedicated to him. I created his altar one Sunday, then I made a collage of all our pictures and hung them another Sunday. I mustered the energy to drink a glass of wine and watch our wedding video by his altar, and I found something every Sunday. I also sought out and joined a widow's group, which ultimately led me to this anthology which has also helped in this process. I continue to talk to Shallah as if he is still physically with me. His altar is well taken care of by me. His urn is in a glass case that I place his favorite foods on top of and light a candle daily. This ritual of still taking care of him also helps in my journey. I now feel more confident and less afraid. I have taken up a self-defense class and started back traveling. Because I talk to my husband regularly, I feel as though he is traveling with me. The support of my mother-in-law and brother-in-law has also been a tremendous help in me not blaming myself. We communicate every week and see each other periodically. For my husband's 1st heavenly birthday, we planned a party at the park. We plan to create a yearly legacy to honor him.

Going through this painful process has led me to realize that no one thing fixes it all. Not all therapy or magic tricks will erase this pain. There will constantly be ebbs and flows of emotions. I had to realize that no one's opinion of what I chose to do matters. No one knows what I went/am going through and cannot place judgment. I also learned to balance my alone time with the support of loved ones. There were many times I just wanted to be alone but being around loved ones helped ease my mind and remind me of the feeling of joy. There are many ways to maneuver through this pain of never physically getting my husband back. Multiple resources can be and should be used simultaneously. I find myself outgrowing some resources and returning to others. I listen to myself and trust that this process does not have a timeline or an end date. It is a continuous process. You may experience periods of anger, loneliness, loss of memory, lack of concentration, and struggle with your new identity. Many people will ask to help you, and you may not be able to tell them what you need. There may be moments when you feel you are getting better, and you get ambushed with the grief you cannot control. It is best to know these periods are expected, and they will not last forever.

I had to rediscover myself and find new interests and people to talk to and hang out with periodically while also keeping my alone time to talk to my husband and watch television shows as though he was still here. You have to be willing to accept help and let your support system know how you feel. Let your support system know if you need help with your children so you can get a night to cry or be by yourself. Whether it be financial assistance, legal advice, household repairs, assistance with your husband's possessions, etc., do not hesitate to ask for help because everyone will understand—those who genuinely want to help will. Many support groups will help you connect with other widows and build a sisterhood. The important things to remember are that you will never stop loving your husband, and the price of love can, unfortunately, be painful.

There is no quick fix, and every emotion you go through is valid because it is yours and how you grieve, but please do not get stuck there. Do not compare your grief to anyone else's, and do not let anyone else compare your grief. You cannot travel this journey alone. Please do not isolate yourself. Remember to love and take care of yourself first. This is a journey, not a sprint. Be patient with yourself and understand this new you.

> *"Don't confuse your path with your destination. Just because it's stormy now doesn't mean that you aren't headed for sunshine."*
>
> *-Unknown*

CHAPTER 7

Pain to Purpose

Teressa Green-Clark

Blessed or those who mourn, for they shall be comforted:
Matthew 5:4

As you continue to read this book, I pray that you will find peace and assurance that life can be revitalized after loss. The death of a loved one leaves a wound that will take time to heal. Grief brings unwanted moments when we look in the mirror and can't recognize the person staring back. After the sudden loss of my husband, I realized I was now in an unfamiliar world. On April 4, 2020, my whole life changed. My sweet husband of three years and ten months transitioned to be with God. As much as I didn't want to accept that his physical life was over, I had to. In life, there will always be situations that we can't understand. For me, I lost a sense of purpose. I was so sure my husband would grow old with me I never stopped to ask myself: *"What would I do if he passed away?"* Now, I'm pondering all kinds of questions concentrating on one in particular: *Why did this happen*? I can vividly replay all the surrealistic encounters of that day.

I was watching television as I let my husband rest up for his last work night of the week. I heard him snoring, so I was sure he was okay. A few hours later, he rose to use the bathroom. As he was walking to the bathroom, he said, *"Babe, I can't feel my left side."* I immediately walked over to him and made sure I heard him say what he said. He repeated it, but this time, he looked at me and said, *"I probably just slept on it too long."* I think he saw the worry in my eyes. I asked, *"Are you sure?"* He said, *"yes, baby, I'm okay."* Just like he sensed my feelings, I felt his as well. He laid back down for a couple of more hours. I heard him get up, so I went in to see if he was really okay. I asked him how he felt. He looked at me and said, *"I still can't feel my left side."* Of course, I panicked. He was calm, doing everything not to worry me. He started dressing for work when he stumbled a little. I screamed, *"Be careful; you sure you're okay?"* He seemed confused. I said, *"You can't go to work like that."* He kept saying, *"I'm okay, but my head hurts."* I walked to the car with him to ensure he was okay as I watched him leave for work. My discernment was telling me he was not okay. He just didn't want me to worry. Whenever we would talk about death, I would get hysterical and cry and ask him, *"Why do we keep having the conversation about death?"*

As I think back on those moments, I wondered, was he sick and he didn't tell me, to protect my heart from hurt? My women's intuition set in. I called the job because something just wasn't sitting right in my spirit. By the time I called, he should have made it and gotten in his truck to deliver his first load of the night, but when I contacted his boss to see if he made it safely, I got the news that he hadn't even started up his truck. I hung up and called his Mom, his kids, and his brother. Your adrenaline sets in when you are scared and nervous, and you don't care about anything. I usually don't go out of my house after he leaves for work, especially if it's not daylight. It was still somewhat dark but almost light. I grabbed my car keys and drove the route he took to work. I didn't see the car by the side of the road, so I thought, okay, this could be good or bad. As I reached the exit to his job, a train had stopped on the tracks. I couldn't cross to see if my husband was in the parking lot at his job. I sat there for as long as I could, scared, nervous, and distraught, to see if the train would move; unfortunately, it didn't after at least 45 minutes. It took everything in me not to get out of my car and crawl under the train to see if my husband was okay. Needless to say… he wasn't.

Intellectually, we may understand that death is a part of the human experience, but is that something we want to deal with? **NO**. Is it something we have to deal with? **Yes**. We cannot run from it or ignore it. Although we can't be prepared or plan for death, we can decide how to address it. This new journey has taught me to allow GOD to bring me from darkness into the light. I remember I didn't want to interact with anyone. I just wanted to be by myself. One of my biggest struggles was trying to attend church without having a meltdown. The way I overcame this fear was by attending another church to see if I felt any emotions. Sure enough, I did. I tried it again and again until there were no signs of emotional grief. When I finally went back to our church, I was more ecstatic than anything. It made me feel good to be back in the place where we both loved going together. I'm learning to take over grief instead of grief taking over me.

I have stumbled into many obstacles along the way. I have experienced shock, guilt, numbness, and, most of all, slight depression. Grief has a way of knocking us off our feet at any given moment. Some obstacles had me scratching my head and trying to make sense of it all. I asked myself, how do you plan to get back up from the challenges that have knocked you down? I prayed heavily and allowed myself to grieve. Whenever I would cry, I would let my emotions take their course, and when it was over, I felt better. I've learned to take the bitter with the sweet. Each day was a different day for me. The most frustrating part of my loss was learning how to sleep at night. I took various sleep aids for help. Even after taking them for a while, I still couldn't sleep sometimes. When I couldn't sleep, I would journal and put my pain on paper. The pain birthed purpose I couldn't imagine inside of me. Grief is never a good feeling, but GOD will allow you to tap into your purpose in pain. Writing became one of my stress releasers. I wrote a letter every day to my husband to help release my emotions. I always kept a pen and notebook with me, even when I went out to handle business.

Doing things in honor of your loved one will help you feel better about yourself. I made a *'remembrance of'* page on social media. On that page, friends, family, loved ones, and I share memories of him. Another tricky time on this journey is the Holidays. I remember decorating our entire place with a different color scheme each year. When my husband transitioned, I wasn't in the Christmas spirit whatsoever. I trained my mind to cope with the intense emotions that would try to consume me. I would listen to a favorite song or think of something fun we would do for that particular Holiday. That worked well for me, but again, each person copes differently. For example, I dressed up and went to our favorite restaurant on my first birthday without him. I thought I was going to be sad, but I actually wasn't. Sometimes you may find yourself feeling left out of everything. I searched grief groups and counseling to help me along the way. I suggest you allow yourself to get into those types of groups because they really help you get peace of mind. I have met so many new friends from groups that I have formed a sisterhood with. It may not look like it or feel like it, but it is possible to transform grief into positive energy. I recommend you find your own unique way to convert your grief into positive energy. Some of the ways I did it were by helping others, praying, and self-care. Self-care is the most essential form of power you can use to help you on this journey. Go out and treat yourself to lunch and a spa day every now and then. As time has passed by, the pain has begun to feel lighter.

This process has empowered me in many different ways. I woke up one morning and decided I was ready to renew myself. I was tired of the constant crying and sadness. I was prepared to take back my life. I wrote a book entitled **"Maximizing my Praise Through Grief"** and started my own business in the middle of a pandemic.

That motivated me and drew me closer to GOD because none of that would have been possible without Him. As widows, I believe we all deserve to wake up in the morning with great excitement about the day ahead of us. I started spring-cleaning my emotions to live a happy and joyous life in which I am so deserving. I put away those emotions that were preventing me from going forward. I started to discover the things that made my heart happy. I found safety in GOD's word. By doing so, I wrote bible scriptures and spiritual quotes on sticky notes and put them all around my house. {Ex: Faith, hope, be encouraged... words of that nature} I would read them three to four times a day to help motivate myself. As the songwriter Donald Lawrence said, sometimes you have to encourage yourself. I did just that. I refused to let the devil steal my joy.

Although this journey can become challenging at times, the love GOD has for me and His generous doses of grace He gives me is indescribable. And although this new way of life is very different, it pushes me to find my purpose through the pain. I am currently working on many upcoming projects, one being WOW - Words of Wisdom Mentoring Service - this service will center on young girls, ages 12-18. I also have a second mentoring service that will be coming later as well. Being able to put together a book and a mentoring service for me is proof that during a storm in your life, you can overcome anything. Even though grief brings many uncertainties, there is a renewed life awaiting us on this journey. Once I started making decisions with my wants and needs, I started piecing myself back together again. You have to think of yourself and what's best for you on this journey. I started learning who I was and which direction I wanted my life to go. You have to give yourself grace. As much as I wanted to go back and change what happened if I could have, it just wasn't happening. Do what helps to make your soul shine. When I wrote my first book and started my business, my soul and willpower were charged like a battery. I'm beginning to give myself more self-talk and beginning to challenge myself outside of the comfort zone I was in. When thinking about giving up, think of your loved one and how everything he couldn't do can be lived out through you.

> *"But seek ye first the Kingdom of GOD, and His righteousness and all these things shall be added unto you"*
>
> *-Matthew 6:33*

A Prayer to You

Dear Heavenly Father,

For every set of eyes reading this, I pray for peace for them. Overtake their lives like never before. I command every stronghold, every heartache, and pain, to loosen that grip from them. May You bind up all plans that the adversary has over their mind, body, and soul. Give them total restoration and freedom on this journey. The loss of their loved ones will not define who they are. Where there is void, fill it, GOD. Where hurt is, I pray You heal them. No longer will they be defeated in the enemy's eyes. Their Past will not determine their future. Help them to find every purpose in this pain. You have for them. I decree and declare it is done in your son JESUS' name.

Amen.

Breathe Sis, this is just a chapter in your book, not the story.

> *"Tough times never last, but tough people do."*
>
> **-*Unknown***

CHAPTER

The Loss After the Loss

Evelyn Donelson

Many people don't realize what goes on after you lose your husband. There are many other aspects to the loss. One being losing your identity as a wife. As in my case, when you lose your husband, you can lose your identity of being a daughter-in-law and even some extended family. I will never know why this happened, and it's not my job to figure it out. I'm only responsible for *"The After."*

I used to be able to call his mother "Ma." There was no judgment felt on the other end of the call. I honestly don't know what happened. It would've been different if we were on bad terms before Lonnie passed. She gave me helpful advice about food and resting after my health scare. It felt so good to have another mama to talk to. Many tell me not to think about the loss after the loss so much. But it's hard. Not only did I lose my husband, but I also lost the other half of my family. That is double grief! My therapist recommended I write them letters. In the beginning, I even thought about contacting Iyanla Vanzant's *"Fix My Life"* show. I don't think about it as much anymore. I've gotten used to not having them around. I believe the pandemic helped a lot. We were hit with the shutdown a few months after the funeral; no visiting family and friends. So, we wouldn't have been able to do the things we would have usually done anyway, such as Memorial Day or 4th of July BBQ and Fireworks.

We went from being one big happy family to being absolutely nonexistent. Looking at our wedding pictures, you would think Lonnie and I birthed all our children together. The truth is our children were grown when we met, but they got along so well people thought they grew up together. We both were against confrontation, and we really wanted everyone to be OK with blending and becoming one family.

My husband made sure that happened. He was always on the BBQ grill and inviting folks over for a quick bite. It lit up his world when he could feed his family and enjoy the laughter and chuckles coming from inside the house. It didn't matter to him if someone brought more meat to put on the grill. It didn't matter if we didn't have any sides to go with the meat. It didn't matter if it took him the entire day to finish cooking. As long as he could see the happiness and everyone getting along well. My husband was family-oriented, and his passion was making sure everyone was happy. His sister became my sister. My brother became his brother. His mother was my "Ma," and my mom became his mama D. We claimed all 9 grandchildren until we started losing count (chuckle). We never viewed our family as two separate ones, but two combined and intertwined. We became one even before the wedding.

I want to take you back to when we made the decision to become one.

Lonnie lived in the west suburban area of Chicago, and I lived in the suburban area of Indiana. It was about an hour to an hour and a half apart, depending on the day. He would come to hang out and play cards and have game night with us, and my daughter would make her famous nachos. He met my mom and the boys, and believe it or not, everyone got along. He asked my mom and kids for their OK to date me. We started hanging out more and more. I wasn't working then, so I had a lot of free time. I was recovering from foot surgery and walking with my ugly boot. I would meet him at the park near the Museum of Science and Industry, which was the halfway mark to his house. Because we would leave so late, he wanted me closer to Indiana. I talked about my kids, and he spoke of his. And we talked about one day becoming one. In my mind, I was thinking five to seven years down the line. When he asked me, *"Would you ever get married again?"* My response was, *"Maybe, one day. It's not on my mind right now."* I finally met his kids. He met my brother, and I met his sister. The next thing you know, he was proposing. It had been a little over a year, and we had conversations about wanting the same things. We discovered that we shared so many of the same interests and had so much in common. We both were in disbelief to learn that butter pecan was our favorite ice cream, blue was both our favorite color, and Martin was our favorite sitcom. No one could tear us apart. We went everywhere together. When he wasn't with me, my family would ask, *"Where's your other half?"* People even started calling us Martin and Gina.

When I lost my husband, I lost my best friend, my better half. I trusted him after everything I went through. We were like Bonnie and Clyde. He used to joke with me about needing a new body when we got older because everything was all broke up. I used to joke and tell him that when he turned 90, I would hit him upside his head with his cane because I just knew we would grow old together. I just knew God wouldn't make me a widow again at such a young age. *Who would have ever thought that my knight would leave me not even a full seven years after the first loss? Who would have thought I would lose another husband, and I'm not even at retirement age?* I didn't think I could handle a loss after a loss, but here I am, writing about it. This was a topic I used to avoid, as if reality wasn't presented before me. I never wanted to talk about losing another husband! And not only am I writing about it, but I also talk about it on talk shows and in daily conversations.

Let me explain why losing after a loss is so difficult.

My offer was accepted for a house. I sent my daughter the videos from the tour, and she texted me and said, *"Lonnie would love the basement and have fun in it."* I went back and watched the video again and tried to hold the tears in, but they just flowed. I'd been so excited about getting a confirmation I didn't even think about how my husband was a handyman, and he loved to fix on and fix up things. It wasn't until my daughter said something that I then pictured him in the basement with all of his tools, building something. When we were on FaceTime, I kept trying to look in the camera, and I just kept putting my head down. My daughter kept saying, *"Mom, it's OK! Hold your head up. He's smiling down at you, and he's happy. You worked hard for this moment, so let's enjoy it."* I lost a moment to share the news with my husband. I didn't experience the joy of sharing the phone call and feeling ecstatic with my life partner. The pleasure of being a first-time home buyer and celebrating a dream come true with my significant other was lost. I lost that moment of feeling we had accomplished one of our goals. I genuinely don't feel 100 percent complete. It feels like a piece of me is missing, and although being a homeowner is what I've strived for, it was a goal WE shared.

The most challenging part is accepting that the person I was finally building something with is no longer here. I think back to those days we would sit in the park and share commonalities, such as being homeowners, entrepreneurship, and working toward retirement. I was finally walking into the image of being a wife again, Lonnie's wife! He was my biggest supporter, my biggest fan, and my life coach. He pushed me when I wanted to give up. He motivated and encouraged me to be that courageous woman he met and courted.

Even though he is not here to see my growth, I can feel his presence when pushing through. I can hear his voice when I feel weak and weary. He would always tell me, *"I didn't marry a wimp."* And that would always make me stop crying. I continue to think about that courageous woman he always stood behind at every event, looking so proud. Yes, I spent many nights on the floor, curled up in a fetal position. And not to mention the crying spells in the grocery store. I cried so much it felt like I ran out of tears. I lost another husband. I lost my extended family, but I wasn't about to lose my mind, my dignity, nor my self-worth. One day, I told myself, *"Focus on winning and what's going to help heal my heart. No more! Yes, you lost a lot, and you're tired of losing. But now it's time to gain."*

I've always said, *"You don't die with your loved one."* And it was time that I started living the words I spoke. In the words of Sarah Jakes Roberts, *"Girl, Get Up!"* I pulled myself up and climbed to the top of that mountain, raised the flag, and vowed to live. I created a routine for myself that helped in the journey I needed to regain my strength. I began to walk into my peace as I started appreciating more in life. I pushed myself to love the *new* I was walking in. I was no longer a wife, but I was still a daughter, a mother, a grandmother, a professional, a CEO, and a caring person who had a desire to help others. So, I decided to do something with all of that, live for my WHY. I prayed for guidance and asked God to order my steps. And He did just that!

He placed in my spirit to start the business I talked about with my husband. I started a nonprofit organization and named it Evelution Inc. Our mission is to help those who are broken and seek healing and transformation. Many of our participants are those who have experienced domestic violence or loss. I became a certified life coach. I help faith-based women evolve into strong leaders that God created them to be. I have appeared on many talk shows and podcasts and even hosted my own webinars and workshops. I've completed two more book collaborations, started my consulting business, and branding into being the motivational speaker I've always wanted to be. My husband would have been right here cheering me on. It would mean so much to get those lost moments back, but I know he is here with me in spirit. I can feel his presence and picture his big smile every time I accomplish something. I know he would've been so proud of me. That motivates me to do more!

The big question is, *"What do you do when you lose other aspects of your life after you lose your husband?"* Well, you adjust. You adjust to not having that particular thing in your life, just as anything else you lose. It is not the same as losing a cellphone or a wallet, but it's the same concept. You accept the loss, adjust to not having that person around, and you appreciate your new. I am no longer a wife but a widow. A widow is a woman who lost her spouse (husband). I am no longer someone's daughter-in-law. I lost my mother-in-law when my husband died. She chose to disown and disassociate herself with me for her own personal reasons. I never had a chance to have that conversation with her or even get clarity from others. I've been told, *"Death change people."* Or *"Death brings out the ugly in people."* I've even heard, *"They're treating you like they've always felt."* That's definitely a hard pill to swallow, but I am doing well with or without my ex-extended family.

I have accepted my losses and moved forward with LIVING. I continue to write and take ownership of being an author. I run my business as my late husband would have wanted me to, smiling and content. And I've adjusted to my new. I can't live in the past and try to fix what's not there. But I can definitely accept what is! Think about it, when you lose your phone and report it lost, the first thing they ask is, *"Is the phone damaged or lost?" "If you have the phone, can it be fixed?" If you lost the phone, it is recorded as a "complete loss."* It can't be fixed because it is no longer in your possession. I've realized that our relationship cannot be restored because it is no longer there. It has been over a year that we've had contact. I miss family gatherings, but with the new that I'm walking in, there will be gatherings in my new home, in my new season! There will be more celebrations of the many gains. Life is about fulfilling the purpose given to you. I believe my purpose is to help others through their loss and make sure that my new light shines bright on everyone who crosses my path. What an awesome thing to help others see.

If you've lost after your loss, be at peace with what has happened in your life. The longer you hold on, the longer it will take to go through the grieving process. You will build up so much anger, hurt, and frustration it will soon start to interfere with your home and work life. Release, let go and live! Appreciate the life God has given you, **be brave and walk in your new.**

Outro
VICTORIOUS WIDOW

Precious S. Brown

As a little girl, you may have longed for the day that you would become a wife. Mainly because we were told to *"grow up, go to college, get a degree, get married, have a family, buy a home with the white picket fence, and life will be complete."* For the most part, many of us really did strive to reach those goals, especially getting married.

The wedding day is always the happiest moment in a woman's life. It is full of fun, family, memories being created, lots of good food, gifts of course, and all the people that love you and your mate. In the process of the vows, you both agree to love each other unconditionally, always be there to support each other, and the pastor typically wraps up with - *until death do us part*. As a little girl, you never understood how important those last few words were - ***"until death do us part."*** For many of us, it wasn't until the loss of the one we loved did we understand the magnitude of the vows we took on the wedding day.

Although I haven't lost a spouse in the natural sense, I have lost a spouse through divorce. So, I won't lie and say I completely understand what the authors of this book have gone through, but I can imagine it is almost parallel to having your heart ripped out of your chest without anesthetic because that is precisely how I felt my season.

The heartache and pain associated with the loss of a spouse are indescribable and, for the most part, unbearable. The emotions are endless. Your thoughts run ramped. Your focus is off. You are lost, and it seems as though it will never end. But as with any trauma, time is required to recover, regroup, restore, and reassess where life is right now compared to where you want life to be.

The hard truth of the matter is life will continue to go on. And at some point, you will have to make the decision to live despite the loss. *Why?* Because you understand that in *living*, you have the opportunity to have fun, make and share more memories, as you grow into the person you were created to be. In that allowing you, in turn, begin to operate at your highest capacity to serve someone else who is in the space in which you were not too long ago. And over time, you will become more aware of the power you possess. Not because you lost your spouse but despite you losing your spouse.

So, as you close this chapter of the book, I employ you to remember your spouse that you loved so greatly. Remember the times you shared, the family you created, the businesses you built, the dreams that you realized and shared together, the vacations you took, or the vacations you wanted to take (*go take it*). But most importantly, remember that you can still have it all in your present time, even though it may feel like you have lost it all.

How do I know? Because you chose to be victorious when it was more befitting to be a victim.

You Are A Victorious Widow!

AUTHOR BIOS

Keisha Heard - Baking and corporate America was her life, but she knew her calling was more. She has always known her calling was more. Always being compassionate for people, specifically hurting and broken people. Always willing to help others despite her own pain and struggles. She always knew something was bigger in store for her but never knew what the destination was or even the process it was going to take to become that person. Completing culinary arts school in 2010 and then completing her certification in management in 2014, she was determined to take the corporate world by storm. But even in climbing through different organizations and companies, she still felt unfulfilled. Losing her husband on March 29, 2019, from alcoholism forged her into using all the compassion and needing to help people and learning how to put it to use. A fire lit inside of her to help people who were struggling with addiction. She became motivated to help people who have identity issues as well.

People who were not sure why they were created or what their next is? She shows people how to navigate through the most painful times in their lives and helps them find purpose. Turn pain into power. She has also had her struggles with infertility, losing 2 kids at an early age. And losing her husband on the day, she was supposed to start IVF also inspired her to help other women with infertility and let them know there is hope at the end of the rainbow. She intends to bring hope to millions of women and men and inspire change. To be a road map for someone else's healing.

As a determined individual, self-starter, encourager, and go-getter, *LaTasha Hicks* remains persistent through every trial and battle she faces. Despite the many challenges, she has consistently exemplified the epitome of winning over every warfare. As a minister in her church and a youth advocate, LaTasha takes pride in helping others and acknowledging others for their accomplishments. She is often known for being "too nice" and has a kind & sweet demeanor.

LaTasha will let nothing, or no one distract her from accomplishing her goals in life directed by God. Her ministry work started back at her college, where she was led to hold a college campus outreach service with the help of her church. In addition to this, she has had the opportunity to conduct a female bible study on her campus. She is a 911 survivor of the World Trade Center and has shared her story in her local community & in her church.

Some of her other works within both business and ministry that led to her birthing season include the following:

- a 2014 Top Performer's Award Recipient in her workplace
- Event Planning & Entrepreneurship Certification
- 2nd Runner Award Recipient in the Jabberwock Pageant of Delta Sigma Theta Sorority
- Former Guest Speaker of the Dr. Kishma George i96 Gospel Radio Show
- Urban Women's Ministry of Wake County Member
- And presently, the Founder and President of W.O.W. Winning Over Warfare Resource Ministries, LLC, which is designed to aid individuals with resources for grief support and inspiration.

To discover more about LaTasha and her business, go to www.wow-winningoverwarfare.com. You can also reach her directly at latasha2541@gmail.com or winningoverwarfare@gmail.com

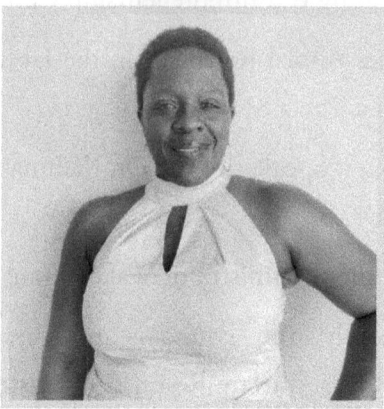

Dr. Sandra McGowan-Watts serves as a family medicine physician and business owner. She was born and raised in Chicago, IL. She attended Lindblom Technical High School. She attended Bradley University and earned a Bachelor's degree. Sandra has always had a passion for science and has been inquisitive. Combining this with her strong desire to help others, Sandra realized her calling was a career in medicine. Sandra graduated from the University of Illinois at Chicago College of Medicine. She completed her training at Steiger Hospital of Cook County.

Dr. McGowan-Watts has dedicated her life to working in medically underserved communities. Her philosophy is to provide care for the "whole" person. Sandra is passionate about forming bonds and making connections with her patients. She loves to work as a team with her patients, helping them better care for themselves.

After 10 years of working for a medical organization, Sandra decided to pursue a lifelong dream. With the help of her husband and family, in January 2019, she stepped out on faith and started her own medical practice, McGowan Family Health & Wellness Center. This journey has been tedious yet rewarding.

Although medicine has brought joy into her life, Sandra is most proud of her family. On October 14, 2007, Sandra married Steven Watts. Sandra's husband and children have provided so much help in becoming who she is today.

Life has been challenging for Sandra. In May 2020, Sandra lost her husband Steven to COVID. Steve's death shook Sandra to the core. At that time, Sandra realized how short life is and that we need to live our true calling. Through this trial, she continued to keep her practice going, as she knew that is what God wants, and this is her and Steve's legacy. In all of this, Sandra remembers what the Bible says in Jeremiah 29:11: "For I know the plans I have for you," declares the Lord, "plans to prosper you and not to harm you, plans to give you hope and a future."

You can contact her at: mcgowanfamilyhealth@gmail.com.

Dr. Debra Pope Johnson is a survivor. She is a breast cancer survivor of 19 years, and she survived the sudden death of her husband in 2012.

She retired in 2018 with 25 years of service in Education in the State of Georgia, teaching 6-12 social studies in the Dougherty (Albany, GA) and Randolph County (Cuthbert, GA) School Systems. Additionally, she served as Curriculum Supervisor for grades 3-12 Social Studies in the Dougherty County Schools System. She was an Instructional Technology Specialist, Adjunct Professor, and Director of Clinical Experiences at Georgia Southwestern State University in Americus, GA. Dr. Johnson has held/or currently holds membership in the following organizations: Georgia Retired Teachers Association, AARP, Georgia Association of Educators, Professional Association of Georgia Educators, National Council of Social Studies, Georgia Council of Social Studies (she served four years as a Trustee), ASCD, National Association of Middle School Teachers. She holds a lifetime membership in Delta Sigma Theta Sorority, Inc. and is presently a member of the Albany (GA) Alumnae Chapter.

Dr. Johnson lost her husband, Frank Johnson Jr., on April 21, 2012. This one event continues to shape her as an individual, and her work as her God-given purpose continues to evolve. Propelled by this loss, Dr. Johnson is a member of many Facebook widow(s) groups and subscribes to several Blogs related to loss, grief, and recovery. She is also an administrator of a Grieving Hearts Facebook Group. Additionally, she continues to mentor widows of all ages and stages as a result of this.

She has two adult daughters (Tolaison Hooks Spence, 39, and Ashley Michele Johnson, 36, two granddaughters (Elle Mckinzley Hooks, seven and Olivia Nicole Spence, three of who are the love of her life. She is actively involved in all their lives.

Pamela Cheatom was a senior Operations Manager of Loss Mitigations for a Major Mortgage Banking Corporation. In that role, Pamela developed or modified training to teach staff best practices. Educated team members on best practices of daily operations as well as company policies. Trained staff on how to resolve customer complaints in a diplomatic, tactful way. Pamela turned attention away from Corporate America in 2011 to raise her family full time. Pamela holds a bachelor's degree in Business Administration Management, Florida Tech.

Raised in Los Angeles, California, Pamela now lives in Lancaster, California. She has raised four children, all of which are grown. Currently, Pamela has five grandchildren. She was also instrumental in assisting her husband in starting a non-profit organization, a church, Christ Family of faith, and served as First Lady and church administrator. Pamela currently enjoys spending an abundance of time with her grandchildren; three boys and two girls. Most of all, nurturing them, assisting in taking care of them, and positively influencing them in any way possible. Pamela believes in Jesus Christ as her redeemer, her peace, strength, comfort, and Joy. Pamela's proudest Moments are being a wife to her late husband, mother to her children, and grandmother.

Khalilah Richardson began this journey of widowhood in November 2020. Not knowing what to do, she turned to a widow's group for support. Through that support group, Khalilah was able to feel empowered and compelled to share her story in hopes that it would help another widow.

Khalilah is the proud mother of two teenagers. She has a 15-year-old daughter who loves fencing, musicals and is beginning drivers Ed and a 13-year-old son who loves anime and creating stories. Throughout the school year, Khalilah divides her time between engaging and teaching pre-k students in Baltimore City to ripping and running her teenagers around to their frequent activities while ensuring their success in school. The summer months are usually dedicated to family travels and bonding.

Khalilah loves to travel to different places every summer, both nationally and internationally. When she is not traveling, Khalilah loves to listen to music in the house and dance. She loves music from the late 90s but also enjoys a variety of different genres. Before the pandemic, Khalilah was actively enjoying club cycling. Club cycling is the combination of listening to music while exercising on a still bike to the beat of each song. This was perfect for Khalilah because it combined her favorite listening activity while she also worked out.

In the past, Khalilah has been a part of many community activities that involve knowledge of oneself, building up the youth, and community connection. Although she still supports these organizations, she is not as active a member as she once was. She hopes to reconnect with those communities, as well as others, soon. Khalilah's late husband volunteered his free time as a youth football coach who inspired many young boys well into their manhood. As part of her husband's legacy, she plans to stay involved with his league and reward a yearly trophy named after her husband to that teams' coach of the year.

Teressa Green-Clark is the fifth of seven children. She grew up in the little town of Drew, Mississippi, in the deep South. She was raised in a home with two loving parents who trained her up in how she should go.

She earned her Associate Degree in Early Childhood at Mississippi Delta Community College. She furthered her education and received her Bachelor of Art in Early Childhood degree at Delta State University in Cleveland, Mississippi. She has worked in education for over seven years, gaining experience in different types of educational teaching that will help shape the little minds of children ages 3-5 years of age. Teressa is passionate about teaching her students and making a difference in their young lives and being an influencer that will produce future generations.

Teressa is also involved in Mentoring Young Girls. She is the owner of TC's Closet LLC., which was launched in February of this year. She has written an Inspirational Guide, which was inspired after the loss of her husband. She wanted to share some of the tools she used to help herself on her grief journey. She is also in the process of launching her WO W. Mentoring Service {Words of Wisdom} by the end of this year or early next year.

Outside of her job, Teressa loves reading her Bible and studying the Word of GOD. She has added another hobby to her list, which is journaling. She encourages others who are grieving the loss of a loved one. Teressa believes GOD chose her to sit on this platform alongside other widows to help pave the way and speak out for grieving souls who can't speak for themselves.

Evelyn Donelson is an Educator with over 20-years of experience in the field of Education and Leadership. She has over 10 years of experience with training and speaking to large audiences and facilitated virtual webinars and Live Stream Videos. Her passion is helping those who are seeking healing find their way back to "life."

She was inspired to start a nonprofit organization, Evelution, that empowers, strengthens, inspires, and builds the life skills of people who suffer from brokenness. As a Domestic Violence Survivor and a two-time widow, Evelyn encourages others to overcome their own battles.

Evelyn exuberates entrepreneurship as a life coach and motivational speaker. Her goal is to travel, speak to the broken, and guide individuals to be great leaders, living the purposed and planned life they are called to live. She is also a co-author of four book collaborations and plans to continue sharing her stories through her writings.

NOTES

www.ingramcontent.com/pod-product-compliance
Lightning Source LLC
Chambersburg PA
CBHW051947160426
43198CB00013B/2341